## MUKER (ABOVE)

**MUKER IS THE LARGEST OF THREE VILLAGES IN UPPER SWALEDALE**, an old lead mining settlement of the 19th century. Originally founded by Norse settlers, the name Muker comes from the Norse *mjor-aker* meaning a small piece of land. The river Swale rises near here, fed by a number of streams tumbling down from the Cumbrian border to the west. A road from Muker leads across the high moors to Wensleydale, via the **BUTTERTUBS PASS** (opposite, above).

# YORKSHIRE DALES FROM ABOVE

## Contents



## Introduction

**From the Vale of York westwards**, the land gradually rises steadily upwards along broad ridges to the high fells of the Pennines at well over 600m. In between the ridges and fells are the Yorkshire Dales: one of the prettiest parts of England. In the 10th century Norse settlers moved eastwards across the Pennines into the Dales from Cumbria, bringing with them their tradition of pastoral farming. Many of the local names for landscape features such as beck, clint, crag, fell, gill, mere, moss, rigg, scar and tarn are derived from ancient Norse influences.

The landscape was sculpted by Ice Age glaciers smoothing hillsides and scouring valleys until they finally retreated around 10,000 years ago. Some 330 million years ago, the area was covered by a shallow tropical sea where many animals lived and died depositing their shells and skeletons on the sea floor. Here they formed layers of sediment that would eventually be compacted into the limestone so characteristic of the Dales. In places, the Ice Age glaciers scraped the limestone clean, exposing it to centuries of rain which ate into the surface forming runnels and fractures. These are the famous limestone pavements of Malham and the terraces of Ingleborough.

The Northern Dales are distinctive: from the town of Richmond with its Norman castle at the eastern end, Swaledale reaches up towards the western fells. The sides can be steep and rocky, but the valley basin is a world of small fields divided by stone walls in geometric patterns, stone field barns, and colourful meadows full of wildflowers. Wensleydale is serene and grassy, famous for its cheese, with beauty spots at Bolton Castle and Aysgarth Falls.

Each of the Dales has its own character: Coverdale, Garsdale, Dentdale, Wharfedale, Ribblesdale, Nidderdale, Teesdale, Littondale, Rosedale, Bilsdale, and more. Each has its share of unspoilt, picturesque villages and serene landscapes: the brilliant greens of the fields in summer, the sparkling water of tumbling streams, and the muted tones of heather and bracken on the fells.

Higher up are the Howgill Fells, Brimham Rocks, Buttertubs Pass, Hardraw Force, and the Three Peaks. Each of them is spectacular. We hope that the photographs in this book will show that the Yorkshire Dales are worthy of further exploration.

Photographs from top to bottom: Arten Gill Railway viaduct, Studley Royal Water Garden, Gouthwaite Reservoir, Swaledale


Photographs, text and design by Adrian Warren and Dae Sasitorn



MYRIAD BOOKS LIMITED

## Richmond Castle (above)

**Richmond Castle, overlooking the River Swale,** was built by the Normans in 1071. Still standing among the ruins is the Great Tower, or keep, which was built in the 13th century and rises to a height of more than 30m. Except for skirmishes with Scottish raiding parties, Richmond Castle has seen very little fighting. It is one of the oldest of all English castles but it was in ruins by the 16th century.

## Swaledale near Crackpot (right)

**The river Swale is one of the fastest flowing rivers** in England. Its name is of Anglo-Saxon origin and is thought to mean "swirling" river. Here is a typical Yorkshire Dale scene near the village of Crackpot: fields divided by stone walls in geometric patterns, stone field barns, and brilliant green meadows at the height of summer. Higher up, in the distance, the colour becomes more muted where heather covers the fells.

## Buttertubs Pass (above)

**Buttertubs Pass is a high mountain road** which leads across the moors from Muker and Thwaite in Swaledale to Hardraw (famous for the high waterfall of Hardraw Force) and Hawes in Wensleydale. The road passes by a cluster of fluted limestone potholes, known as the "Buttertubs". Tradition has it that, long ago, farmers would suspend their butter and cheese in sacks overnight in the deep, cool, rocky fissures of the Buttertubs before resuming their long journeys to market.

## Oxnop Scar (left)

**Oxnop Scar is a stretch of exposed limestone** on the flank of a wild pass between Swaledale and Wensleydale. It crosses the watershed at 498m above sea level.

## **Bainbridge** (above)

**The Romans came to Bainbridge** in about AD80 and established a succession of forts nearby, one of which can be seen to the left of the village in the photograph. In the Middle Ages the village stood on the edge of a large forest. The Bain, England's shortest named river, flows for just 3km (2 miles) from Semer Water down through Bainbridge to join the river Ure.

## **River Ure** (right)

**The River Ure is one of the larger rivers** draining off the eastern flanks of the Pennines. It flows from the uplands of the Yorkshire Dales through Wensleydale to the low-lying fertile plains in the Vale of York. East of Hawes, the river wanders lazily across a wide flat valley floor. The photograph shows an extreme meander between Middleham and Leyburn.

## Semer Water (left)

**Semer Water, just south of Wensleydale**, is the largest natural lake in Yorkshire and is a haven for wildfowl. It was formed during the last Ice Age when a retreating glacier deposited a moraine which acted as a dam. In 1937, a Bronze Age village was found beneath the waters when the lake was being drained for a land reclamation scheme.

## Leyburn (below)

**Leyburn is the main commercial** centre in Wensleydale. It is a prosperous market town with some attractive 18th-century buildings and wonderful views of nearby Wensleydale.

## Bolton Castle (above)

**Situated in a prominent position near Leyburn**, in Wensleydale, Bolton Castle is a spectacular medieval fortress. It was built in 1378 by Richard le Scrope, 1st Lord Scrope of Bolton and Lord Chancellor of England. The castle looks out over the beautiful dales, but where there is now heather or bracken, in the 14th century it was covered by forest. In 1568 Mary Queen of Scots was held prisoner at Bolton for six months before being moved to Tutbury Castle. Remarkably, Bolton Castle has never been sold, and remains in the private ownership of the 7th Baron Bolton, Richard le Scropes' descendant.

## Middleham Castle (left)

**An 11th-century motte and bailey castle** here was abandoned in the 12th century when a new castle with a massive stone keep was built. The keep is one of the largest in England and, unusually, it incorporates the great hall. A stone curtain wall was built in about 1300, and in the 15th century the castle was transformed into a comfortable residence. It became home to some of the greatest lords of the time, including Salisbury, Warwick and Richard, Duke of Gloucester, later Richard III.

## Jervaulx Abbey (above)

**Jervaulx was founded by John de Kinstan** in 1156 for the Cistercian order following a vision of the Virgin Mary and Child nearby. The church has suffered severely and little now remains but the ground plan. Here at Jervaulx as elsewhere, following Henry VIII's dissolution of the monasteries, stone was plundered to construct houses. The ruins are a little overgrown, but because of this it is extremely atmospheric. Jervaulx is privately owned, although open to the public.

### Brimham Rocks (above)

**Brimham Rocks, a short distance from Pateley Bridge** in Nidderdale, are scattered over some 50 acres. The elements have fashioned the rocks into fantastic shapes that seem to defy gravity and resemble faces and animals. Made of tough sandstone known as millstone grit, most of the rocks owe their bizarre shapes to erosion during and after glaciation when moving ice and, later, windblown sand wore away the softer layers in the rock strata.

### Ripon (right)

**Ripon dates from the 7th century** and is one of England's smallest cathedral cities. Its impressive cathedral was built during the 12th and 13th centuries and stands on the site of an Anglo-Saxon church which was destroyed in 950. Ripon is known for its historic buildings and was a cloth and lace-making centre in the Middle Ages. A horn blower sets the watch nightly in the market square at 9pm carrying out a traditional ceremony said to be 1,000 years old.

### **Fountains Abbey** (LEFT)

**St Mary of the Fountains was built** in the 12th century, founded by monks who had left York in 1132 and adopted the Cistercian code. The site was remote and wild, purposely chosen to underline their wish for a stricter rule. The magnificent ruins bear testament to the skill of the masons who came from Burgundy. The long, vaulted cellarium, over 90m long, survives little altered since its construction, its ribbed vault supported by 19 central pillars. At the east end of the church, a huge transept was built.

### **Thornborough Circles** (ABOVE)

**The unparalleled cluster of three ancient** interconnecting henges at Thornborough, North Yorkshire, is of international importance comparable to those at Stonehenge and Avebury. Together with other local Neolithic-Bronze Age monuments, the circles represent an important religious centre for people living here between 4000 and 2000BC. The circles are massive, with a maximum diameter of about 244m. The northern one covered by trees is the best preserved, while the other two have been ploughed repeatedly.

### **Ingleborough** (OVERLEAF)

**At 723m, Ingleborough, with its famous flat-topped** profile, is perhaps the best known of the famous "Three Peaks", the other two being Whernside and Pen-y-Ghent. The summit plateau is the site of the only Iron Age hill fort in the Dales. The limestone pavements in the foreground were caused by glaciation during the last Ice Age. As the ice moved it scraped away surface layers to expose the limestone underneath to erosion by centuries of rainfall, cutting a criss-cross network of channels called "grikes" and isolating blocks called "clints".

## Pen-y-Ghent (left)

**The "Three Peaks" of Whernside**, Ingleborough and Pen-y-Ghent dominate the skyline. Geologically, the Three Peaks are all of millstone grit capping a limestone base. Pen-y-Ghent, at 693m, towers over Ribblesdale and the head of Littondale. The Pennine Way long distance footpath passes over the top of Pen-y-Ghent, the peak forming the watershed of the Pennine fells: water flows west into the River Ribble and east into the Rivers Wharfe and Aire.

## Masham (right)

**Masham, pronounced "Mass'm"**, is a market town at the edge of the Dales in Wensleydale. Its importance as a centre increased during the Middle Ages through the influence of nearby Fountains and Jervaulx Abbeys. Masham is known for its annual sheep fair held annually at the end of September. During the 18th and 19th centuries this was one of the biggest in the north of England with up to 70,000 sheep filling pens in the market square.

## Pateley Bridge (left)

**Pateley Bridge is situated** amid the patchwork of green meadows and drystone walls in Nidderdale. The Romans mined lead near here. In the 14th century it became a market town and later a centre for the flax and linen industries powered by water from the river Nidd. It is now a centre for agriculture and tourism, and Upper Nidderdale has been designated an Area of Outstanding Natural Beauty.

## Gouthwaite Reservoir
(LEFT)

**Gouthwaite reservoir** was built in 1899 to supply water to Bradford via an aqueduct. Unfortunately its creation caused the inuncation of Gouthwaite village and its Elizabethan hall. The River Nidd feeds the reservoir which has become a highly prized bird sanctuary, home to a wide variety of waterfowl. It has been designated as an SSSI (Site of Special Scientific Interest).

## Angram and Scar House Reservoirs

**Angram Reservoir** (above) and **Scar House Reservoir** (left) were built to supply water to the Bradford area. Scar House took 15 years to complete and was finally finished in 1936. Stone for the reservoir dam was quarried from the two sites which can still be seen on either side of the valley. During the construction of Scar House reservoir a village was built just below the dam to house the workforce.

## Skipton Castle
(RIGHT)

**A Norman castle of earth and timber** was built here on a cliff above the Eller Beck by Robert de Romille in about 1090 and was later rebuilt in stone. In 1310 Edward II granted the castle to the Clifford family. The inner curtain wall with six towers forms a D shape enclosing a courtyard surrounded by early Tudor buildings. During the Civil War the castle withstood a three-year siege by Parliamentary forces and it was partially demolished to prevent any further military use. In 1659 Lady Anne Clifford planted a yew tree to mark the completion of her restoration work following the Civil War.

## Kettlewell (RIGHT)

**Kettlewell is a small village** at the foot of Great Whernside in Upper Wharfedale. The name is Anglo Saxon and comes from *cetel wella* which means bubbling spring or stream, and signs of Anglo-Saxon farming methods are still visible in terraced fields to the south of the village. Kettlewell is famous for its dry stone walls which were built in the late 17th and early 18th centuries. Lead mining and the cotton industry have played an important role in the history of the village.

## Conistone Moor (LEFT)

**Upper Wharfedale's scenery** is dominated by the Great Scar Limestone of the Craven Pennines, and throughout the valley white scars of rock mark the hillsides such as here on the fells above the village of Conistone. These sometimes form spectacular outcrops such as Kilnsey Crag next to the village of **Kilnsey** (page 24).

## Kilnsey (above)

**Kilnsey is a small village in Wharfedale**, most famous for its proximity to Kilnsey Crag, an impressive overhanging limestone cliff and one of the main attractions for rock climbers in the Yorkshire Dales. The Kilnsey Show is a leading northern agricultural show held on the Tuesday after the August Bank Holiday in the shadow of the crag.

## Grimwith Reservoir (right)

**Grimwith is the largest reservoir in the Yorkshire Dales**, surrounded by high moorlands between Grassington and Pateley Bridge. It was created in 1864 and enlarged during the 1970s to seven times its original size. Some parts of Grimwith are important breeding areas for waterfowl and it is very popular for sailing and windsurfing.

## Grassington (left)

**Grassington is the metropolis for Wharfedale**, a large village with charming cobble-stoned lanes and stone cottages. Bronze and Iron Age settlements have been found north of the village, and the surrounding landscape shows evidence of two thousand years of farming. Lead mining brought prosperity to Grassington in the late 18th and early 19th centuries.

## BOLTON PRIORY (LEFT)

**CANONS OF THE ORDER OF ST. AUGUSTINE** settled here in Wharfedale in 1155. Now in ruins, the setting in riverside meadows surrounded by hills is superb, and has inspired many artists including Turner. Many of these works show the walls overgrown with ivy and other plants. Bolton is one of several monasteries established in Yorkshire during the 12th and 13th centuries.

## LITTONDALE (RIGHT)

**LITTONDALE IS DRAINED BY THE RIVER SKIRFARE** and is one of the few valleys in the Dales not to be scarred by lead mining. Stone walls and stone field barns decorate the valley floor. Many of the villages, such as **ARNCLIFFE** (pictured right) trace their history back to the Anglo Saxons who favoured well-drained gravel sites for their settlements. Then, much of the land was covered by forest. Limestone dominates with scars visible along the hillsides.

## BARDEN TOWER (RIGHT)

**THE FOREST OF BARDEN WAS A HUNTING GROUND** for the owners of Skipton Castle. In the late 15th century, Henry Clifford, the "Shepherd Lord", rebuilt one of the hunting lodges and made it his principal residence. During the Wars of the Roses he spent his youth in the Cumbrian fells tending sheep, hiding from the Yorkists who had killed his father and grandfather. In 1658, Lady Anne Clifford of Skipton restored the decaying property. Following her death it was taken over by the Earls of Cork, but fell into decline in the late 18th century.

## Malham Tarn
(RIGHT)

**A natural upland lake, Malham Tarn** lies on a floor of impervious Silurian slate approximately 400 million years old. The tarn was dammed by a moraine from the retreat of the ice-sheet at the end of the last Ice Age. In 1791 the level of the tarn was raised by Lord Ribblesdale who constructed a dam and weir. The tarn was granted to Fountains Abbey by William de Percy in the 12th century, together with all its fishing rights. The tarn has a reputation for fine trout.

## Otley (LEFT)

**Otley, in Wharfedale**, lies at the foot of a 275m-high hill called the Chevin. It is an agricultural market town and the annual agricultural show each May is claimed to be the oldest of its kind. Thomas Chippendale was born here in 1718 and Turner painted many scenes in the local area.

## Malham Cove (RIGHT)

**Malham Cove is a huge natural limestone cliff** just north of Malham village. It was once the site of a spectacular prehistoric waterfall. The land above the cove is now dry, the river having found an alternative route through a cave system underground. However, at the foot of the cliff, a small stream called Malham Beck rises from a submerged cavern, which is still being explored by cave divers. The vertical face of the cliff is about 80m (260ft) high, at the top of which is a large area of limestone pavement.

## Settle-Carlisle Railway

**Completed in 1876, the Settle to Carlisle Railway** is England's most scenic railway and was the last mainline railway to be built. With 115km (72 miles) of track, 17 major viaducts and 14 tunnels the landscape presented a tremendous challenge to the engineers. At upper Dentdale the track emerges from Blea Moor Tunnel to cross two viaducts – Arten Gill and Dent Head. **Arten Gill viaduct** (left), with 11 arches, 36m high, 200m long, is the larger, and is built of massive blocks of Dent "marble", from the now-disused quarries nearby. **The Ribblehead viaduct** (above), with 24 arches, 32m high, 400m long is the most impressive structure on the railway.

## LAST REFUGE Ltd

Nature is a precious inheritance, to be cared for and cherished by all of us. Last Refuge Ltd is a small company primarily dedicated to documenting and archiving endangered environments and species in our rapidly changing world, through films, images and research. The company was established in 1992 for a study of wild giant pandas in the Qinling mountains of central China, which seemed, literally, to be the "last refuge" for these charismatic animals. The company continued to embrace new projects worldwide. Two films on lemurs in Madagascar quickly followed and the ring-tailed lemur became the company's logo. Adrian Warren and Dae Sasitorn, who run the company from a farmhouse in Somerset, have created a special website, www.lastrefuge.co.uk, in order to present their work. This is becoming a huge resource for information, and an extensive photographic archive of still and moving images for both education and media. Ultimately they hope to offer special conservation awards to fund work by others.

## ADRIAN WARREN

Adrian Warren is a biologist and a commercial pilot, with over 30 years' experience as a photographer and filmmaker. He has worked worldwide for the BBC Natural History Unit, and as a director in the IMAX giant screen format. He has recently designed a new wing-mounted camera system for aircraft to further develop his interest in aviation, aerial filming and photography. As a stills photographer, he has a personal photographic archive of over 100,000 pictures, with worldwide coverage of wildlife, landscapes, aerials, and peoples. His photographs appear in books, magazines, advertisements, posters, calendars, greetings cards and many other products. His awards include a Winston Churchill Fellowship; the Cherry Kearton Medal from the Royal Geographical Society in London; the Genesis award from the Ark Trust for Conservation; an International Prime Time Emmy; and the Golden Eagle Award from New York.

## DAE SASITORN

Dae Sasitorn is an academic from the world of chemistry but has given it up to follow her love for the natural world. She manages the company and is a computer expert. She has created, designed and manages the Last Refuge website as well as scanning thousands of images for the archive. She is also a first-class photographer in her own right.

## THE PHOTOGRAPHY

Adrian and Dae operate their own Cessna 182G out of a tiny farm strip close to their house. They bought the single engined four-seater aircraft in May 1999 in order to develop a new wing-mounted camera system for cinematography. The 1964 Cessna was in beautiful condition, and had only one previous owner. It is the perfect aircraft for aerial work: small, manoeuvrable, with plenty of power, and the high wing configuration offering an almost unrestricted view on the world below. With 20 degrees of flap it is possible to fly as slowly as 60 knots. The cabin side window opens upwards and outwards and is kept open by the airflow. The photographs were taken on Hasselblad medium format 6 x 6 cm cameras and lenses using Fujichrome Velvia film. Waiting for the right weather, with a clear atmosphere and less than 50 per cent cloud cover, required being on standby for months.

**First Published in 2004 by Myriad Books Limited,**
**35 Bishopsthorpe Road, London, SE26**



**ISBN 1 904154 85 9**

**Designed by Dae Sasitorn and Adrian Warren**
**Last Refuge Limited**
**Printed in China**